OVERCOMING ADVERSITY:
SHARING THE AMERICAN DREAM

GEORGE CLOONEY

MASON CREST PUBLISHERS
PHILADELPHIA

OVERCOMING ADVERSITY:
SHARING THE AMERICAN DREAM

OVERCOMING ADVERSITY:
SHARING THE AMERICAN DREAM

GEORGE CLOONEY

DANA HENRICKS

MASON CREST PUBLISHERS
PHILADELPHIA

ABOUT CROSS-CURRENTS

When you see this logo, turn to the Cross-Currents section at the back of the book. The Cross-Currents features explore connections between people, places, events, and ideas.

Produced by OTTN Publishing, Stockton, New Jersey

Mason Crest Publishers
370 Reed Road
Broomall, PA 19008
www.masoncrest.com

First printing

1 3 5 7 9 8 6 4 2

Library of Congress Cataloging-in-Publication Data

Henricks, Dana.
  George Clooney / Dana Henricks.
      p. cm. — (Sharing the American dream)
    ISBN 978-1-4222-0600-3 (hardcover) — ISBN 978-1-4222-0741-3 (pbk.)
    1. Clooney, George. 2. Motion picture actors and actresses—United States—Biography—
Juvenile literature. I. Title.
    PN2287.C546H46 2008
    791.4302'8092—dc22
    [B]
                                        200805

OVERCOMING ADVERSITY:
SHARING THE AMERICAN DREAM

TABLE OF CONTENTS

CHAPTER ONE

FOLLOWING A DREAM

George Clooney discovered his calling at the age of 20, when his uncle José and cousins Miguel and Rafael visited his hometown of Lexington, Kentucky. The three hadn't come to Lexington for a holiday visit, a birthday, or a wedding. Rather, they had come to shoot a movie. George's uncle José was José Ferrer, an Academy Award–winning actor. George's cousins Miguel and Rafael Ferrer were themselves beginning careers as actors. All three Ferrers had roles in *And They're Off*, a film about horse racing.

George Clooney had always been close to his cousin Miguel. When Miguel invited him to drop by the set of *And They're Off*, George decided to go. The film's producers ended up renting George's car for $50 a day. They also gave him a part in the movie as an extra. George was hooked.

Miguel told him he should move to Los Angeles to be an actor. "I had just spent the summer cutting tobacco, which is a miserable job," George Clooney recalled many years later. Going to Hollywood seemed like an excellent idea.

Hollywood Dreams

Pursuing his newfound dream of becoming a movie star would require George to abandon his former career plans, however. After

George Clooney, who followed a youthful dream to become a movie star, is one of Hollywood's leading luminaries.

high school, George had enrolled at Northern Kentucky University, where he studied broadcast journalism. That was a field in which George's father had made a big mark, as a TV news reporter and an anchorman.

When Nick Clooney found out about George's plans to go to Hollywood, he tried to talk his son into remaining in school. "At least with a diploma, you'll have something to fall back on," he told George, according to Nina Clooney, Nick's wife and George's mother.

"If I have something to fall back on, I'll fall back," George replied.

Though George had made up his mind to go to Hollywood, he didn't have enough money to make the move. He went back to cutting tobacco. He also took other jobs. He sold women's shoes at a department store. He drew caricatures of people at a mall and ran a lemonade stand during a Labor Day festival.

By the fall of 1981, George was ready. He climbed into his '76 Monte Carlo and, with $300 in his pocket, set off for California to become a movie star.

George was no overnight sensation in Hollywood. He discovered that, famous family or not, becoming a star requires hard work, perseverance, and in many cases luck. George toiled for a dozen years before getting his big break. In the meantime, he struggled constantly to make ends meet. For a while, he lived with a friend who had offered him a spare closet as a bedroom. "I can still remember sitting on the closet floor of my buddy's house, completely broke," George told an interviewer in 2005. "My friends would want to go out to dinner, to get a hamburger, and I couldn't afford to go. They had the money to pay, but I didn't want them to pay. That happened a lot."

George landed a few small TV and movie roles. He also took on a variety of odd jobs outside of the entertainment industry.

George Clooney as pediatrician Doug Ross in *ER*, the hit TV series that launched him to stardom. George appeared on the show five seasons, beginning in 1994.

These included doing construction work, selling insurance, and drawing caricatures.

In the end, the struggle paid off. In 1994, George got a role on the TV series *ER*, which became a hit. He would receive two Emmy Award nominations for his work on the show. George later successfully made the transition to the big screen. He has appeared in blockbuster movies as well as films that have won critical acclaim. As of 2008, George had been nominated for four Academy Awards, and he had won once—as Best Supporting Actor for his role as a CIA agent in 2005's *Syriana*.

Today, George Clooney is one of the most highly respected members of the TV and film industry. He seems believable playing just about any role, from a kindly doctor to a charming con artist, a cool detective, a brooding gangster, or even a bluegrass-singing hillbilly. But George has won respect for much more than his acting.

Humanitarian Mission

George Clooney is deeply involved in a variety of humanitarian causes. Among them are providing aid to people displaced by violence, and focusing the world's attention on large-scale violations of human rights. In 2006, George and his father traveled to the African countries of Sudan and Chad. There they heard firsthand accounts of atrocities committed against the people of Darfur, a war-torn area of western Sudan.

READ MORE

Conflict in Darfur has produced one of the worst humanitarian crises of the 21st century. For details, see page 44.

In 2007, after his return from Africa, George took action. Along with fellow actors Brad Pitt, Matt Damon, Don Cheadle, and David Pressman and movie producer Jerry Weintraub, he founded the organization Not On Our Watch. Its first act on behalf of Darfur was a $2.75 million donation to the International Rescue Committee (IRC), an organization that provides relief to refugees. Since then, Not On Our Watch has worked with the IRC and other humanitarian organizations to provide health care, improve living conditions, and increase the safety of victims of the violence in Darfur.

The actor tours the headquarters of the United Nations' peacekeeping mission in El Fasher, in the Darfur region of Sudan, 2008. George Clooney has been a vocal advocate for ending the violence in war-torn Darfur.

In January 2008, George Clooney was named an official United Nations Messenger of Peace. In announcing George's new title, Secretary-General Ban Ki-Moon told the actor, "You have seen first-hand the pain experienced by the victims of war and made it your personal mission to help end violence and human suffering."

READ MORE

For a brief description of how the United Nations was formed, and what it does, turn to page 45.

George Clooney has complained loudly about the celebrity press, which frequently intrudes into his private life. But he also recognizes that celebrity has an upside: it provides him unique

Before the January 28, 2008, ceremony naming him a UN Messenger of Peace, George Clooney is joined by his father, Nick; his mother, Nina; and Dr. Asha-Rose Migiro, deputy secretary-general of the United Nations.

opportunities to help other people. "I am right where I want to be in life," he told a *Rolling Stone* reporter in 2007. "I'm having dinner in two nights with Bernard Kushner, the French foreign minister, and we're working on a Darfur policy. I want to be able to do that. I'm not a policymaker, but I'm an advocate—maybe a little more than an advocate."

His family, friends, and countless fans around the world would agree that George Clooney is a little more than an advocate. Much more.

CHAPTER TWO

A KENTUCKY BOY

George Timothy Clooney was born in Lexington, Kentucky, on May 6, 1961. He was the second child of Nina and Nick Clooney. George's sister, Adelia (known as Ada), had been born the year before. Nina Warren Clooney, George's mother, was a former state beauty queen.

Nick Clooney's career as a newscaster took him to a variety of radio and television stations throughout Kentucky and Ohio. As a result, the Clooney family moved a lot during George's early years, and he had to change schools often. He started first grade at Blessed Sacrament School in Fort Mitchell,

A high school yearbook photo of George Clooney.

Kentucky. Then he went to St. Michael's School in Columbus, Ohio. Next he attended Western Row and St. Susanna schools,

A good athlete, George played basketball and baseball at Augusta High School in Augusta, Kentucky. He was even invited to try out for the Cincinnati Reds professional baseball organization.

both located in Mason, Ohio. Finally, he began his high school years at Augusta High School in Augusta, Kentucky, where he graduated in 1979.

It can be tough to change schools a lot and always be the "new kid." George's first year at Augusta High School was made even harder when he came down with Bell's palsy, a condition in which a facial nerve is paralyzed. This makes it impossible to control the muscles on one side of the face. Because of the disease, George could not move the left side of his face. He couldn't keep his left eye open, and it was hard for him to eat or drink. The other kids at school teased him mercilessly about it. Later, George saw this as an important experience because it made him a stronger person. He learned not to take himself too seriously. He also learned to poke fun at himself first and thereby beat other people to the punch.

The Bell's palsy went away after about a year, and George

was able to play sports, which he loved. He was on Augusta High's basketball and baseball teams. George dreamed of a professional baseball career, and he was talented enough to attract some interest from the Cincinnati Reds. He was invited to a pair of tryouts in 1977, when he was 16. The experience dampened his visions of baseball stardom. "When I was young, I thought I'd be a professional baseball player," he recalled. "I was good. I had two Reds tryouts, but when I went up to bat, the pitcher threw an eighty-five-mile-an-hour curve-ball at my head, and I threw myself to the ground. Everybody was laughing. I remember standing up, and it was the first real-ization that I wasn't going to be a professional baseball player. It was devastating."

Famous Family

Pursuing a career in show business did not occur to George early on. This may seem odd, given how successful some of his family members were in the entertainment field. Rosemary Clooney, George's aunt, was an enormously popular singer and actress. In addition to recording four songs that hit #1 on the Billboard charts, she was a film and TV star. Her movie credits included the beloved 1954 musical *White Christmas*, with Bing Crosby. Rosemary Clooney had been married to veteran film and TV actor José Ferrer, whose role in the 1950 movie *Cyrano de Bergerac* had garnered him an Oscar for Best Actor.

Despite his family connections to Hollywood stars, George eyed a different career as he approached graduation from high school. He planned to follow in his father's footsteps and take up broadcast journalism.

Nick Clooney's broadcasting career had begun at age 16, when he started working for radio station WFTM in Maysville, Kentucky. His TV broadcasting career included jobs as news reporter and news anchorman. He also hosted popular talk-show programs in Cincinnati and Columbus, Ohio. When George was only five years old, Nick would take him to the TV studio and allow him to appear briefly on camera during the shows.

Throughout his career, Nick Clooney was a strong supporter of social activism. He encouraged his two children to be concerned about human rights as well. He would often quiz George and Ada about important social activists, asking them who Martin Luther King Jr., Bobby Kennedy, and Malcolm X were and what they had done.

Nick also insisted that George read one book a week and write a book report about it. At first, George found this to be a tedious chore. "But then I read *To Kill a Mockingbird*," he later recalled, "when all these big issues were coming to a head, especially the civil rights issue. I realized that a book could change the world."

After graduating from high school, George enrolled in Northern Kentucky University, which is located a few miles southeast of Cincinnati, in Highland Heights, Kentucky. After being bitten by the acting bug, however, George abandoned his plans for a degree in broadcast journalism and set out for Hollywood. He figured he could get a little help from his aunt Rosemary.

Los Angeles

Rosemary Clooney did help George—at first. Though she was not thrilled when George showed up on her doorstep practically broke and without any job prospects, she took him in and gave him a place to stay. She also provided him with a job—not as an actor, but as a driver on her nationwide concert tour.

After the tour ended, George tried finding work as an actor but had no luck. The lack of success began to take a toll on his disposition. George became difficult to be around—so much so that his aunt asked him to move out. Fortunately, his friend

Rosemary Clooney, 1954. George's aunt was a popular singer and actress.

In his long career as a broadcaster, Nick Clooney, George's father, had numerous radio and television jobs. Here he is seen as a disc jockey for the U.S. Armed Forces Network, during a fund-raiser to combat polio.

Tom Matthews gave George a place to stay. But his home was no luxurious Hollywood mansion. Like George, Matthews was struggling to make it in show business, and all he had to offer his friend was a walk-in closet. Still, it was better than nothing, so George spent a year sleeping in the extremely cramped quarters of his friend's closet.

This hardship did not deter George from pursuing his dream of becoming an actor. He worked construction and did odd jobs to support himself, all the while auditioning for TV roles and commercials. During this time, George also took acting classes with the legendary drama teacher Milton Katselas. But for many years, the only roles George managed to land were bit parts in TV shows or low-budget B movies.

CHAPTER THREE

BIT PARTS AND B MOVIES

By the mid-1980s, George Clooney was landing plenty of TV roles. They just weren't the kinds of roles he wanted. George appeared in single episodes of such forgettable series as *Riptide*, *Street Hawk*, and *Throb*. From 1984 to 1985, he had a recurring if minor role in the short-lived hospital situation comedy *E/R*. He played an emergency-room doctor named Ace.

After *E/R* was canceled, George moved on to play a small role on *The Facts of Life*, a popular sitcom about a group of young girls at a boarding school. His character, handyman George Burnett, appeared in 17 episodes of the show, from 1985 to 1987.

In 1988, after his run on *The Facts of Life*, George landed another small recurring role. This time he played factory boss Booker Brooks on *Roseanne*, a comedy show about a lower-middle-class family.

To this point in his career, George had played only minor roles. Yet a hallmark of his acting had already begun to emerge: George's ability to make whatever character he played seem real. "He breathes believability into his roles," comedian Roseanne Barr, the star of *Roseanne*, would later tell *Time* magazine, "because he's real where it's hardest for actors to be: in

A scene from an episode of *The Facts of Life*. From 1985 to 1987, George had a small recurring role on the sitcom. He played a handyman.

life. Somehow he manages to be cool, handsome and a stand-out while keeping that regular-guy thing going."

B-Movie Bonanza

Whether George Clooney was able to "breathe believability" into his early film roles is highly debatable. But that had as much to do with the quality of the scripts as the quality of George's acting.

In 1987's *Predator: The Concert*, George appeared alongside such big-name actors as Charlie Sheen and Louise Fletcher. But the real star of the movie was the giant grizzly bear that, angered by hunters, creates mayhem at a rock concert held in a national forest.

A serial killer was on the loose in the sophomoric *Return to Horror High*, in which George had a small part as a policeman. The movie was released in 1987.

The following year, George could be seen as a young man scheming to pick up women in *Return of the Killer Tomatoes!* Though campy by design, *Killer Tomatoes!* was, in the view of most critics, simply dreadful.

Difficulties Personal and Professional

If George Clooney didn't seem to be making much headway toward his dream of becoming a movie star, he did take a major step in his personal life: he got married. For about a year, George had lived with Kelly Preston, a struggling actress. In 1989, however, the two broke up. Preston left her former boyfriend with something unusual to remember her by: a pot-bellied pig named Max, which George would keep until the pig's death 18 years later.

Right after his breakup with Preston, George reunited with a woman he had dated some six years earlier, actress Talia Balsam. Within four months, they packed up a Winnebago, drove to Las Vegas, and were married.

Over the next few years, George continued working in television while auditioning for major movie roles. In 1991, he landed a role on *Baby Talk*, a TV series based on the hit movie *Look Who's Talking*. He appeared in just four episodes, however.

George Clooney with his girlfriend Kelly Preston, 1988. Max, the couple's pot-bellied pig, is on George's lap.

George got into a fight with the show's director over the director's humiliating treatment of an actress. After quitting the show as a result of that confrontation, George worried that he might never work as an actor again.

That worry proved unfounded. In 1992–93, George played a detective on the crime series *Bodies of Evidence*. The following season he had a recurring role on *Sisters*, a drama that revolved around the very different paths taken by four sisters from Illinois. George played the ex-husband of one of the main characters.

George's modest success on TV wasn't matched on the big screen. He auditioned for some choice roles but, to his frustration, lost out to other actors. George tried out for the part of J.D., a charming but deceitful hitchhiker in director Ridley Scott's *Thelma and Louise*. Although the director had George read for the part five times, he ended up casting a relative unknown named Brad Pitt in the role. Released in 1991, *Thelma and Louise* became a big hit. But George was so upset about not landing the part that he couldn't bring himself to watch the movie for an entire year.

George also auditioned unsuccessfully for a part in *Reservoir Dogs*, a crime film that was being shot by an obscure director named Quentin Tarantino. Tarantino rocketed to fame with the huge success of *Reservoir Dogs*, which was released in 1992 to critical acclaim.

George Clooney, meanwhile, was acting in movies such as *The Harvest*, in which a screenwriter has one of his kidneys stolen in Mexico. George's cousin Miguel Ferrer received top billing in the 1993 film, while George had a bit part as a cross-dressing entertainer.

Along with his career frustrations, George dealt with setbacks in his personal life. In September 1993, after less than four years of marriage, he and Talia Balsam were divorced. "It was my fault all the way down the line," George would later say of the breakup. He vowed that he would never get married again and never have children. (Later, George even made a $10,000 bet with actresses Michelle Pfeiffer and Nicole Kidman, who insisted that he would

READ MORE

For a brief profile of actress Talia Balsam, who was married to George Clooney from 1989 to 1993, see page 46.

be a father by age 40. They lost. When Kidman sent him a check for $10,000, George returned it, telling them to give the money to charity.)

Big Break

In 1994, George finally landed a role that would bring him the stardom he had been seeking for so long. He was hired to play pediatrician Doug Ross on the TV hospital drama *ER*. The series was an instant hit, becoming America's top-rated show and making George Clooney a household name.

George received two Emmy Award nominations, in 1995 and 1996, for his work on *ER*. In 1997, 1998, and 1999, he and the rest of the *ER* cast members won the Screen Actors Guild Award for Outstanding Performance by an Ensemble in a Drama Series. The show went on to become the longest-running hospital drama ever, completing 15 seasons before finally concluding in March 2009.

George, however, had only signed on for a five-year contract. Often when actors make it big on a TV series, they are suddenly

READ MORE

To find out about the Emmy Awards, turn to page 47.

The stars of *ER* accept their Screen Actors Guild Awards for Outstanding Performance by an Ensemble in a Drama Series, February 24, 1997. From left: George Clooney, Anthony Edwards, Gloria Reuben, Noah Wyle, Laura Innes.

flooded with offers to make movies. George was no exception. It is not uncommon for actors to break their TV contracts to become movie stars. George, though, refused to break his contract. He had made a commitment, and he intended to stick to it. When asked about George's decision to honor his contract, George's father, Nick Clooney, told *People* magazine: "I'm prouder of that than I am of his performances. He kept his word."

However, nowhere in his contract did it say that George could not make movies in between shooting episodes of *ER*. And that is exactly what he did.

CHAPTER FOUR

THE MOVE TO MOVIES

Georg Clooney's success on TV's *ER* earned him offers to act in better and bigger-budget films. In 1996, between shooting episodes of *ER*, George starred in *From Dusk Till Dawn*. The action/horror film, directed by Robert Rodriguez, costarred Quentin Tarantino and Harvey Keitel. George's role was quite a departure from the character he played on *ER*, the likable pediatrician Doug Ross. In *From Dusk Till Dawn*, George portrayed a violent bank robber, Seth Gecko. His smoldering performance earned rave reviews.

In another 1996 film, *One Fine Day*, George was back playing a good guy—a divorced newspaper columnist with a young daughter who meets a divorced architect (played by Michelle Pfeiffer) with a young son. Critics generally dismissed the romantic comedy as predictable, if not boring. George Clooney wasn't used to negative reviews. But the critical reception of *One Fine Day* was mild compared with the avalanche of disapproval that met George and his next movie, *Batman & Robin*.

Lessons from a Bad Film

The Batman movie franchise had been highly successful. The Dark Knight's first big-screen outing, *Batman* (1989), had starred

George Clooney as bank robber Seth Gecko in the 1996 Robert Rodriguez film *From Dusk Till Dawn*. The role was a big-screen breakthrough for George.

Michael Keaton in the title role and Jack Nicholson as the fiendish Joker. It was a smash hit. Two sequels, *Batman Returns* (1992) and *Batman Forever* (1995), were also extremely successful. The writers seemed to have gotten the formula down pat: Cast a hunky male star in the role of Batman, fill all the villain roles with A-list actors (such as Michelle Pfeiffer as Catwoman, Jim Carrey as the Riddler, and Tommy Lee Jones as Two-Face), and top it off with amazing costumes and eye-popping special effects.

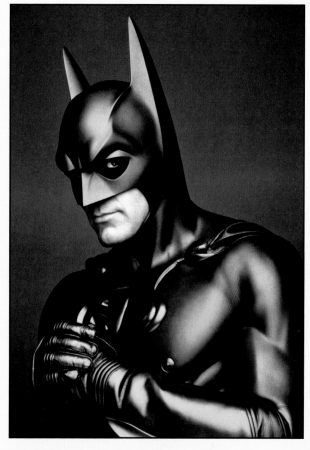

George Clooney wears the bat suit in this publicity shot for *Batman & Robin.* The 1997 movie was mocked by film critics and Batman fans alike.

By the time George Clooney put on the bat suit in 1997's *Batman & Robin*, however, the formula had lost its fizz. Critics panned the movie as silly, tedious, and without substance. "Watching it is like stumbling into the world's longest coming attractions trailer," complained *Los Angeles Times* movie critic Kenneth Turan, "or a product reel for a special-effects house." Turan went on to say that George Clooney had not helped his chances of becoming a movie star with his appearance in *Batman & Robin.*

George didn't dispute the critics' judgment. "It's a bad film," he admitted to *Time* magazine, "and I'm the worst thing in it." Still, the criticism stung.

"I got beat up for *Batman & Robin,*" George told *Esquire* magazine. "Fair enough. I got paid a decent amount for it, and I'm a big kid. I can take my hits. But I was a little surprised how hard I got hit for it and how the hits come when you're not looking."

The experience taught George a valuable lesson: he should choose film roles based not on whether the movie was likely to be a blockbuster but on whether he was genuinely interested in the story line.

Hollywood Superstar

With his newfound insight, George Clooney rebounded from the dismal *Batman & Robin*. He notched a string of critical and box office successes. Critics loved *Out of Sight*, a 1998 film directed by Steven Soderbergh. In it George played an escaped bank robber who develops a relationship with the federal marshal he kidnaps, played by Jennifer Lopez.

In *Three Kings* (1999), George played Archie Gates, an American sergeant major in Iraq immediately after a cease-fire has ended the fighting in the 1991 Gulf War. Gates and three other American soldiers find a map showing the location of a stash of gold stolen from Kuwait by the Iraqi army. The Americans decide to hunt for the gold and steal it for themselves. Along the way, they meet Iraqis who are in serious danger from their own government. The soldiers must decide whether to help these people or to keep looking for the gold. Critics loved *Three Kings*—and George Clooney's performance in it. Jami Bernard of the *New York Daily News* called the movie "a daring, teeth-grinding experience that doesn't let the viewer rest easy." Roger Ebert of the *Chicago Sun-Times* praised *Three Kings* as "some kind of weird masterpiece, a screw-loose war picture that sends action and humor crashing head-on into each other and spinning off into political anger." Of George

Clooney's performance, Ebert said, "Like many natural action stars, Clooney can do what needs to be done with absolute conviction; we believe him as a leader."

George's next big-screen appearance was in another critically acclaimed and popular film: the 2000 comedy *O Brother, Where Art Thou?* In the movie, directed by Joel and Ethan Coen, he plays a slick-talking, bluegrass-singing escaped convict.

In *The Perfect Storm* (2000), based on the nonfiction best seller by Sebastian Junger, George

READ MORE

George Clooney has appeared in three films by Joel and Ethan Coen. Turn to page 50 to learn about these two talented brothers.

returned to a dramatic role. He played the captain of an ill-fated fishing boat.

The 2001 movie *Ocean's Eleven*, a remake of a popular 1960 film, had George playing con artist Danny Ocean. He gathers together a group of endearing criminals to rob a Las Vegas casino. *Ocean's Eleven* connected with moviegoers, grossing more than $450 million worldwide.

George Clooney's film successes allowed him to try his hand behind the camera. In 2002, he directed *Confessions of a Dangerous Mind*. The movie was based on the memoirs of Chuck Barris, the host of the original *Gong Show*, who made the bizarre claim that he was a CIA hit man. *Confessions* received good reviews but did not do well at the box office.

George returned to acting in 2003 in another Joel and Ethan Coen movie, *Intolerable Cruelty*. The comedy costarred Catherine Zeta-Jones.

In 2004, George reprised his role as Danny Ocean in *Ocean's Twelve*. The sequel was considered good but not quite as inspired as *Ocean's Eleven*. Still, it grossed a respectable $362 million worldwide.

Acclaimed Work

In 2005, George Clooney directed, cowrote the screenplay for, and played a small role in *Good Night, and Good Luck*. The film was about the confrontation between journalist Edward R. Murrow and Senator Joseph McCarthy. During the early 1950s, McCarthy accused—without evidence—hundreds of Americans of being communists. His accusations cost people their reputations and their careers. *Good Night, and Good Luck* showed George Clooney's belief in the power of a free press to keep government from abusing its power. The movie received six Academy Award nominations, including Best Director (George Clooney) and Best Original Screenplay (George Clooney and Grant Heslov).

READ MORE

Senator Joseph McCarthy became notorious for his communist witch hunt of the early 1950s. Page 48 has details.

George also acted in another 2005 film with political overtones: *Syriana*. The movie explored the complex and shadowy relationships between U.S. government agencies, oil corporations, and oil-rich countries in the Middle East. George won an Academy Award, as Best Supporting Actor, for his portrayal of a CIA agent in *Syriana*. The accolades came at a price, however. During one scene, in which his character was tied to a chair and beaten, George fell backward and smashed his head on the ground, tearing the membrane that surrounds the spine. Spinal fluid leaked into his body and even out his nose. The accident was extremely painful and led to numerous operations to

George Clooney at the London premiere of *Good Night, and Good Luck*. He directed and cowrote the script of the 2005 film, which garnered six Academy Award nominations.

repair the damage. The injury also caused George to experience short-term memory problems.

The year 2006 reunited George with director Steven Soderbergh for another serious drama, *The Good German*. George played a journalist who is pulled into a murder investigation in post–World War II Germany.

Ocean's Thirteen (2007) provided George a break from the heavy-hitting dramatic roles. The third film in the series wasn't quite as popular as the previous two, though it performed respectably at the box office.

Michael Clayton, also released in 2007, was a serious drama that earned widespread critical acclaim. George portrayed the title character, an unethical corporate lawyer. He earned another Academy Award nomination for Best Actor.

In 2008, George starred in two comedies. *Leatherheads* was about a football team in the earliest days of the sport. *Burn After Reading*, another Joel and Ethan Coen movie, revolved around two employees at a gym who find a computer disk with highly sensitive information on it. They try to extort money from the CIA agent who lost the disk.

A Big Joker

George Clooney's penchant for comedy is not limited to his movies roles. Over the years, he has gained a reputation as one of the biggest practical jokers in Hollywood. George's love of practical jokes may have come from his uncle George, who was constantly telling wild stories and playing pranks on people when George was young. In 2005, George Clooney told *Esquire* magazine about his uncle:

I remember us kids sitting around at this reunion and Uncle George telling stories: "Chick, take off

your finger for George Timothy and Ada Frances."
Uncle Chick had this fake finger, and he'd do one of
these moves and put his finger on the table. "Now,
Chick, take out your teeth." And Chick took his den-
tures out and laid them on the table. "Now, take out
your eye and put it on the table so the young ones
may gaaaaaaze upon it." Chick took out his glass
eye and stuck it on the table. And Uncle George
said, "Now, Chick, unscrew your head." And all of
us kids took off running, because when you're four
years old you believe anything is possible.

One of George Clooney's pranks targeted his friend Richard
Kind. He raved to Kind about the painting class he was taking.
George finally presented a painting to his friend, which he had
found in a trash can but which he said he had painted. The
painting was extremely ugly, but George seemed so proud of it
that Kind felt compelled to hang it in his living room. Only
much later did George reveal where the painting had actually
come from.

George's friends are not the only targets of his practical
jokes. George, like most celebrities, has been harassed by
paparazzi. These photographers stalk famous people and take
pictures and video of them without their permission. George
got revenge on the paparazzi by starting a rumor that his
friends and fellow actors Brad Pitt and Angelina Jolie were
going to be married at George's Lake Como mansion in Italy.
He even went so far as to place tables with umbrellas on his
lawn. The prank worked. The paparazzi descended on his
home by the hundreds. There were even helicopter flyovers. It
took a couple of weeks for the photographers to figure out that
no wedding would take place there.

George Clooney's criticism of the paparazzi prompted celebrity photographers to strike back. Here, at the premiere of 1997's *The Peacemaker*, photographers lower their cameras and refuse to take George's picture.

In 2006, George tried to shut down the Web site Gawker.com, which posts real-time celebrity sightings so that fans can rush to where the celebrities have been spotted. George wrote an e-mail to all his friends and associates, telling them to post fake celebrity sightings on Gawker.com and thereby make it useless. The prank backfired when Gawker.com offered a prize to the next person to take an unauthorized camera phone picture of George.

George Clooney played these pranks on the paparazzi to protest the way they treated stars. George would later go on to confront organizations and even governments over their treatment of ordinary people.

CHAPTER FIVE

MAKING A DIFFERENCE

Nick Clooney played a major role in shaping his son's sense of justice and his desire to make the world a better place. Nick taught George to stand up for what he believes in and to help others who are being mistreated. George has worked for a variety of causes, some affecting people in the entertainment industry, others affecting people in far-off lands.

Taking on the Paparazzi

Some paparazzi will do anything to get a sensational photo of a star. In 1997, Diana, Princess of Wales, and her fiancé, Dodi Al-Fayed, were killed in a car accident in Paris while trying to escape from paparazzi.

George Clooney was enraged and saddened by Diana's death. In 2007, George himself was nearly in an accident when a pushy photographer chased him and his girlfriend while they were out for a motorcycle ride. George decided to take action. He boycotted the TV show *Entertainment*

READ MORE

Page 51 presents a brief profile of Princess Diana, whose untimely death in 1997 saddened millions of people around the world.

George Clooney with girlfriend Sarah Larson at the New York City premiere of *Michael Clayton*, September 24, 2007. Larson had broken her foot in a motorcycle accident in which George suffered a hairline fracture of a rib.

Tonight to protest the "stalkarazzi" techniques of *Hard Copy*, a tabloid TV show owned by the same company that owned *Entertainment Tonight*. George persuaded other actors to join the boycott. Their protest was successful in getting *Hard Copy* to ease up on its pushy tactics.

However, in spite of his run-ins with paparazzi, George remains a strong supporter of freedom of the press. As he told *Time* magazine in 2007:

> I am the son of an anchorman. I am a First Amendment guy. In a statement after Diana's death, I said the only thing worse than out-of-control photographers with no sense of conscience would be to try to restrict them. You can't restrict freedom of speech or the press, even if it's miserable.

Standing up to SAG

But it wasn't just the paparazzi that offended George's sense of fairness. In 2007, television and movie writers went on strike. They believed they were not getting their fair share of the money made when the shows they had written were sold as DVDs, over the Internet, and on cell phones. They refused to work until an agreement was reached that gave them the compensation they believed they deserved.

Most actors supported the writers' strike and refused to work. However, some actors continued to work.

The Screen Actors Guild (SAG), a union that represents professional actors, took action against actors who worked during the writers' strike. Famous guild members who had worked during the strike were fined, but three obscure actors were kicked out of SAG. George Clooney supported the writers' strike, but he was outraged by this unequal treatment. His protests led to SAG's reinstatement of the three lesser-known actors.

Stepping up and Helping Out

On the national and international stage, George Clooney has stood tall in helping people in need. When the United States was reeling from the terrorist attacks of September 11, 2001, George organized the "America: A Tribute to Heroes" telethon. Featuring performances and speeches by stars such as Bruce Springsteen, Mick Jagger, Alicia Keys, Jim Carrey, and Sheryl Crow, the

The actor speaks at a rally intended to pressure the U.S. government to take steps to end the violence in Darfur, Washington, D.C., April 30, 2006.

At the Venice Film Festival, Venice, Italy, August 27, 2008.

telethon raised more than $30 million for 9/11 survivors and the families of victims.

George has also been a vocal advocate for the people in western Sudan's Darfur region. After traveling to the war-torn area with his father in 2006, George testified at a United Nations Security Council meeting and urged the international community to end the atrocities. In 2007, he cofounded the charity Not On Our Watch. Its goal is to raise money to help improve the living conditions of people in Darfur, and to provide humanitarian aid to other people facing extreme oppression around the world. In December 2008, George hosted a fund-raising party in London that collected nearly $15 million for Darfur relief.

What the Future May Bring

George Clooney remains quite busy making movies and promoting causes he believes in. His schedule doesn't easily accommodate a long-term relationship—which George doesn't seem particularly interested in anyway. Over the years, he has dated many women—including French model Céline Balitran; actresses Charlize Theron, Kimberly Russell, and Renée Zellweger; and English model and MTV Europe host Lisa Snowden. But George continues to insist that he will never again marry. "I am never at home," he said in a 2008 interview, "and women get sick of it. . . . I don't expect to ever get married again or have children. I am always working and have so many interests outside acting. If I was them I would never put up with me for long—and they don't."

George Clooney has said he wants to live his life to the fullest. In this, he has been motivated by words his uncle spoke on his deathbed. "Uncle George was sitting in his bed, sixty-eight years old," the actor told *Esquire* magazine.

> He looked at me and said, "What a waste . . ." To this day, I don't know if he was talking about the smoking that destroyed his lungs and barely let him breathe at the end, or the drinking, or if he was talking about his life in general, that he hadn't become the man that all that promise asked him to be.
>
> But I came to the conclusion that I was not going to wake up one day at sixty-five and say, "What a waste." At the very least, I was going to grab as much out of this life as I could.

Darfur

Sudan is the largest country in Africa. Located to the south of Egypt, it is made up largely of harsh and marginal land. The northern part of Sudan is on the eastern edge of the Sahara Desert.

Darfur is Sudan's vast western region. It is ethnically mixed, but in general residents identify themselves as either Arabs or as black Africans. Traditionally, those who considered themselves Arabs made their livelihood as nomadic herders, moving continually in search of grazing land for their camels and other livestock. Those who called themselves Africans were subsistence farmers, growing just enough food to support their families.

The two groups lived in peace for many years. In fact, the farmers would let the nomads water and feed their herds as they passed through the farmers' land. However, after a major drought, farmers blocked off their land to protect it from overgrazing. This created violent conflicts between Darfur's herders and farmers.

The situation became much worse in 2003, after farmers formed rebel groups to demand a greater share of Sudan's resources. The Arab-dominated government responded by arming Arab militia groups in Darfur. With support from the Sudanese military, these militia groups—known as *Janjaweed*, or "devils on horseback"—descended on farming communities. They looted and burned villages, and they brutally raped and murdered residents.

As of 2008, the attacks had destroyed hundreds of villages, left an estimated 400,000 people dead, and forced about 2.3 million Darfur residents from their homes.

Children from Darfur at a refugee camp in neighboring Chad. The conflict in Darfur has claimed the lives of hundreds of thousands of people and displaced millions.

The United Nations

The United Nations is an international organization whose main purpose is to promote peace throughout the world. It grew out of a conference—held in August 1941, during World War II—between U.S. president Franklin D. Roosevelt and British prime minister Winston Churchill. The two leaders released a document called the Atlantic Charter. In it they laid out guiding principles for a more peaceful future after the war.

In January 1942, the United States and the United Kingdom were joined by the governments of 24 other countries in the Declaration by United Nations, which signaled acceptance of the principles outlined in the Atlantic Charter. In June of that year, with World War II winding down, representatives of 50 countries signed the United Nations Charter in San Francisco. In October 1945, the UN Charter entered into force with ratification (or official approval) by 51 member states.

From those beginnings, the UN has expanded dramatically. As of 2008, there were 192 member states.

Today, the UN also has many agencies and branches, including the United Nations Children's Fund (UNICEF); the World Health Organization (WHO); and the International Court of Justice. The UN's goals include conflict resolution and peacekeeping, protection of human rights, aid to refugees and victims of disasters, the preservation of important cultural sites, and more.

The United Nations headquarters in New York City.

CROSS-CURRENTS

Talia Balsam

Talia Balsam has followed in the footsteps of her parents, both of whom were actors. She was born in New York City on March 5, 1959, to Martin Balsam and Joyce Van Patten. Character actor Martin Balsam appeared in such classic movies as *12 Angry Men* (1957), *Psycho* (1960), and *Breakfast at Tiffany's* (1961). He also had a host of TV roles to his credit. Joyce Van Patten was a veteran TV actress.

Talia Balsam got her start in television in 1977, when she appeared in the popular series *Happy Days*. Roles in the prime-time soap opera *Dallas* and the sitcom *Taxi* soon followed. In the 1980s, Balsam appeared on cop and mystery shows such as *Hill Street Blues*, *Cagney & Lacey*, and *Murder, She Wrote*. The 1990s brought roles in *Law & Order*, *Mad About You*, and *Diagnosis Murder*, among other shows. In 2003–04, she appeared in *Without a Trace*. In 2007, she landed a role in the popular series *Mad Men*. Balsam has acted in motion pictures as well, but her films have not been particularly successful.

Balsam married George Clooney in 1989. They were divorced in 1993. Five years later, in 1998, she married actor John Slattery. Together they have one child.

Actress Talia Balsam with her husband, actor John Slattery, 2008.

The Emmy Awards

The Emmy Awards, which honor outstanding work in television, are awarded by the Academy of Television Arts & Sciences (ATAS). That group was founded in 1946 by Syd Cassyd. Cassyd—who became a prolific TV writer, producer, and editor—wanted to promote the new medium of television. The first meeting of the ATAS was on November 14, 1946, in Los Angeles. Only five people showed up. Still, as television grew, so did the ATAS. Today it has more than 15,000 members.

The first Emmy Awards ceremony was held in January 1949. A 20-year-old ventriloquist named Shirley Dinsdale, who starred in a puppet show called *Judy Splinters*, received the first Emmy, for Most Outstanding Television Personality. Other categories included Best Film Made for Television and Most Popular Television Program.

Since then the number of awards categories has expanded dramatically. And now there are two organizations bestowing Emmy Awards: the Los Angeles–based Academy of Television Arts & Sciences founded by Syd Cassyd, which gives out the Primetime Emmy Awards; and the New York–based National Academy of Television Arts & Sciences, founded by variety show host Ed Sullivan, which awards the Daytime Emmys, along with the Emmys for sports, news, and documentary programs.

Jaime Pressley poses with her Emmy as Outstanding Supporting Actress in a Comedy Series, for her role in *My Name is Earl*, September 16, 2007. The Emmys, awarded annually, honor outstanding work in television.

Senator Joseph McCarthy

A U.S. senator from Wisconsin, Joseph McCarthy became notorious for his communist "witch hunt" of the early 1950s. At the time, the United States was engaged in a global struggle with the communist Soviet Union. McCarthy stirred up Americans' fears that many of their fellow citizens were aiding the Soviets. He accused hundreds of Americans, generally without providing any evidence, of being communists.

McCarthy's first target was the U.S. State Department. In 1950, he said he had the names of many "known communists" working in that important government department. By 1952, McCarthy was chairman of an influential Senate committee that investigated supposed communist influence in the United States. His accusations spread to the U.S. army and the entertainment industry.

McCarthy and his allies ruined the reputations of many Americans. Many people accused of being communists were fired from their jobs.

Although many Americans disagreed with McCarthy's tactics, very few were willing to challenge him directly, for fear they too

Joseph McCarthy at U.S. Senate hearings about supposed communist influence in the army, May 1, 1954.

would become victims of his communist witch hunt. In March 1954, however, journalist Edward R. Murrow criticized the Wisconsin senator in a widely seen TV broadcast. A few months later, during televised Senate hearings on communism in the U.S. army, lawyer Joseph N. Welch responded to a reckless accusation from McCarthy by cutting off the senator. "You have done enough," Welch declared. "Have you no sense of decency?"

This proved to be a turning point. McCarthy's power faded. Within three years he was dead of alcohol-related causes.

The Coen Brothers

Joel Coen (born in 1954) and his younger brother Ethan (born in 1957) have won fame as brilliant and multitalented filmmakers. The two, who collaborate on their projects, have directed, written, and produced a string of critically acclaimed movies known for surprising plot twists, quirky characters, and clever humor.

The Coens began their moviemaking careers with the 1984 crime drama *Blood Simple*, which they cowrote and codirected. They followed that up with the critically acclaimed *Raising Arizona* (1987), an offbeat comedy. The crime drama *Fargo* (1996) earned the Coen brothers an Academy Award for screenplay writing. Two years later, the Coens collaborated on another hit, *The Big Lebowski*. That film combined mistaken identity, crime, and comedy.

O Brother, Where Art Thou? was the first Coen brothers film in which George Clooney appeared. It was a big hit in 2000. The movie—inspired by Homer's ancient epic poem *The Odyssey*—was set in the Depression-era American South. It followed the adventures of three bluegrass-singing escaped convicts as they attempt to evade capture and find riches.

Among the Coen brothers' other hits is *No Country for Old Men* (2007). The bleak tale of murderous violence won four Academy Awards. Joel and Ethan Coen shared three of the Oscars, for Best Picture; Best Directing; and Best Writing, Screenplay Based on Material Previously Produced or Published.

Princess Diana

Lady Diana Frances Spencer was born in 1961 in Norfolk, England. In 1981, at the age of 20, she married Prince Charles, the heir to the throne of England, in a fairy-tale wedding watched by millions around the world.

Beautiful and stylish, Princess Diana was a beloved, yet shy, member of the royal family. After she and Charles divorced in 1996, Diana emerged from the shadow of British royalty. She used her fame to call attention to causes she believed in. Diana worked to ban land mines, which are responsible for maiming countless innocent victims in war zones and former war zones. She also supported charitable causes such as AIDS research.

Princess Diana died in a 1997 car crash in Paris. Millions watched Diana's funeral on television, just as they had watched her wedding years before.

Memorials were created to honor Princess Diana's memory. In London's Hyde Park, a memorial fountain was built in her honor. At the Pont de l'Alma tunnel in Paris, where Diana died, a statue already in place was adopted as a memorial to her. Visitors to Paris still show their love for Diana by leaving bouquets of flowers at the statue.

These British postage stamps honor Princess Diana, whose life was cut short by a car accident in 1997.

Chronology

1961: George Timothy Clooney is born in Lexington, Kentucky, on May 6.

1981: Moves to Los Angeles to pursue his dream of becoming an actor.

1984: Lands his first TV series role on the show *E/R*.

1989: Marries actress Talia Balsam.

1993: Marriage to Talia Balsam ends in divorce.

1994: Gets his big break on the TV medical drama *ER*.

1996: Stars in the movie *From Dusk Till Dawn*.

1997: Receives bad reviews for the movie *Batman & Robin*.

1999: Leaves *ER* to pursue a full-time career in movies. Stars in *Three Kings*.

2000: Buys a mansion overlooking Lake Como, in Italy. Appears in the critically acclaimed movie *O Brother, Where Art Thou?*

2003: Makes his directorial debut with the movie *Confessions of a Dangerous Mind*.

2005: Writes, directs, and acts in *Good Night, and Good Luck.* Plays a CIA agent in *Syriana,* for which he wins an Academy Award for Best Supporting Actor.

2006: Makes his first trip to Darfur and is inspired to cofound the charity Not On Our Watch.

2007: Stars in *Michael Clayton.*

2008: Is officially appointed a UN Messenger of Peace. Raises nearly $15 million for Darfur relief.

Accomplishments/Awards
Selected Filmography

From Dusk Till Dawn (1996)

One Fine Day (1996)

The Peacemaker (1997)

Out of Sight (1998)

The Thin Red Line (1998)

Three Kings (1999)

O Brother, Where Art Thou? (2000)

The Perfect Storm (2000)

Spy Kids (2001)

Ocean's Eleven (2001)

Welcome to Collinwood (2002)

Solaris (2002)

Confessions of a Dangerous Mind (2002)

Spy Kids 3-D: Game Over (2003)

Intolerable Cruelty (2003)

Ocean's Twelve (2004)

Good Night, and Good Luck. (2005)

Syriana (2005)

The Good German (2006)

Ocean's Thirteen (2007)

Michael Clayton (2007)

Leatherheads (2008)

Burn After Reading (2008)

Awards

1996 MTV Movie Award, Best Breakthrough Performance, for *From Dusk Till Dawn*

2001 Golden Globe Award, Best Performance by an Actor in a Motion Picture—Comedy/Musical, for *O Brother, Where Art Thou?*

2006 Golden Globe Award, Best Performance by an Actor in a Supporting Role in a Motion Picture, for *Syriana*

2006 Academy Award, Best Performance by an Actor in a Supporting Role, for *Syriana*

2008 Golden Globe Award, Best Performance by an Actor in a Motion Picture—Drama, for *Michael Clayton*

Further Reading

Clooney, George, and Grant Heslov. *Good Night, and Good Luck.: The Screenplay and History Behind the Landmark Movie.* New York: Newmarket Press, 2006.

Cushman, Shana. *George Clooney: The Illustrated Biography.* London: Carlton Books UK, 2008.

Potts, Kimberly J. *George Clooney: The Last Great Movie Star.* New York: Applause Theatre and Cinema Books, 2007.

Internet Resources

http://www.imdb.com/name/nm0000123/

The Internet Movie Database's George Clooney page contains his TV and movie credits, as well as links to a short biography, his awards and award nominations, and news stories.

http://www.notonourwatchproject.org/

The official Web site of Not On Our Watch explains the organization's mission and the humanitarian issues on which it is currently working.

http://www.oscars.org/

The official Web site of the Academy of Motion Picture Arts & Sciences has information about Oscar Award winners and nominees.

http://www.emmys.org/

This is the Web site of the Academy of Television Arts & Sciences, the organization that awards the Primetime Emmys.

Glossary

acclaimed—praised; applauded.

activism—the practice of taking direct action in support of a cause, especially when that cause is controversial.

advocate—a spokesperson; someone who speaks up on behalf of other people or a cause.

atrocities—violent, horrific, and brutal actions carried out against a group of people.

B movies—movies that are made with very small budgets and that frequently are of poor quality.

boycott—to refuse to use, take part in, or be a part of something as a form of protest.

caricature—a cartoonish drawing of a person that exaggerates his or her features.

civil rights—legal rights that a person has as a member of society.

communist—referring to the principles or followers of communism, a political and economic system characterized by complete government control of the economy and, frequently, by repression of citizens under the rule of the Communist Party.

humanitarian—committed to acting in ways that benefit humankind.

paparazzi—aggressive photographers who seek to get candid photos and video footage of celebrities to sell to tabloid newspapers, magazines, TV shows, and Web sites.

sitcom—a TV comedy series that involves a continuing cast of characters; also called situation comedy.

telethon—a fund-raising program broadcast on TV for a specific cause, often featuring celebrities.

witch hunt—a search for, and harassment or persecution of, people with unpopular views.

Chapter Notes

p. 6: "I had just spent . . ." A. J. Jacobs, "The 9:10 to Crazyland," *Esquire.com*, March 17, 2008. http://www.esquire.com/features/george-clooney-0408

p. 8: "At least with a diploma . . ." Nina Clooney, "George Clooney Well-Rooted in N. Ky." http://www.clooneyunlimited.com/george/biography/

p. 8: "If I have something . . ." Ibid.

p. 8: "I can still remember . . ." Cal Fussman, "George Clooney," *Esquire* (January 2005): 63.

p. 11: "You have seen first-hand . . ." Secretary-General Ban Ki-Moon, address to the United Nations, January 2008. http://www.theirc.org/news/not-on-our-watch-0687.html

p. 12: "I am right where . . ." Peter Travers, "George Clooney," *Rolling Stone* (November 15, 2007): 80.

p. 15: "When I was young . . ." Ibid.

p. 16: "But then I read . . ." Ibid., 84.

p. 20: "He breathes believability . . ." Roseanne Barr, "George Clooney," *Time* (May 12, 2008): 108.

p. 25: "It was my fault . . ." Dotson Rader, "It's Finally About Friendship and Loyalty," *Parade* (February 21, 2006).

p. 26: "I'm prouder of that . . ." "George Clooney: Biography," *People.com*, 2008. http://www.people.com/people/george_clooney/biography

p. 29: "Watching it is like . . ." Kenneth Turan, review of *Batman & Robin*, directed by Joel Schumacher, *Los Angeles Times*, June 20, 1997.

p. 29: "It's a bad film . . ." Joel Stein, "Guess Who Came to Dinner?" *Time* (March 3, 2008): 49.

p. 30: "I got beat up for . . ." Fussman, "George Clooney," 63.

p. 30: "a daring, teeth-grinding . . ." Jami Bernard, " '3 Kings' Strikes Gold in the Gulf, *New York Daily News*, October 1, 1999.

p. 30: "some kind of weird . . ." Roger Ebert, review of *Three Kings*, directed by David O. Russell, *Chicago Sun-Times*, October 4, 1999. http://rogerebert.suntimes.com/apps/pbcs.dll/article?AID=/19991004/REVIEWS/910040306/1023

p. 31: "Like many natural action stars . . ." Ibid.

p. 34: "I remember us kids . . ." Fussman, "George Clooney," 58.

p. 40: "I am the son of . . ." "10 Questions," *Time* (October 15, 2007): 8.

p. 42: "I am never at home . . ." Alison Adey, "George Clooney: Women Can't Put up with Me," *NOW* (July 12, 2008). http://www.nowmagazine.co.uk/celebrity-news/265955/george-clooney-women-can-t-put-up-with-me/1/

p. 43: "Uncle George was sitting . . ." Fussman, "George Clooney," 118.

p. 51: "You have done . . ." United States Senate Web site, Historical Minutes, "Have You No Sense of Decency?" October 10, 2008, http://www.senate.gov/artandhistory/history/minute/Have_you_no_sense_of_decency.htm

Index

Numbers in **bold italics** refer to captions.

Photo Credits

About the Author

DANA HENRICKS is a freelance writer and editor living in the beautiful Bitterroot valley of western Montana. Inspired alternately by the Bitterroot and Sapphire mountain ranges and by her two stalwart donkeys, named Lewis and Clark, Dana writes reading passages and questions for standardized tests and test preparation books. *George Clooney* is Dana's first work of biographical nonfiction.